The Future of Technology

How Innovations Are Shaping Our World and Changing Our
Lives

Alina Duncan

1

The Future of Technology

TABLE OF CONTENTS

Chapter 1: Introduction to Technological Innovation

The Evolution of Technology

Technology has been a cornerstone of human advancement, shaping societies and transforming the way we live, work, and interact. From the rudimentary tools of our ancestors to the sophisticated digital ecosystems that define modern life, the evolution of technology is a testament to human ingenuity and adaptability. This chapter delves into the significant milestones in the journey of technological evolution, highlighting the inventions and innovations that have fundamentally altered the human experience.

The journey begins in the prehistoric era, where early humans crafted simple stone tools. These tools, such as hand axes and flint knives, were pivotal in the survival and development of early human societies. They enabled our ancestors to hunt, process food, and protect themselves, laying the groundwork for more complex technological advancements.

As human societies evolved, so did their technological capabilities. The discovery of fire was a monumental leap forward, providing warmth, protection, and a new method to cook food, which improved nutrition and health. The mastery of fire also led to the development of pottery and metallurgy, as humans learned to manipulate materials to create stronger and more durable tools and containers.

The advent of agriculture marked another significant technological milestone. The shift from nomadic hunter-gatherer lifestyles to settled farming communities allowed for the development of stable food supplies and the growth of populations. Innovations such as the plow and irrigation systems revolutionized farming, increasing efficiency and productivity. This agricultural revolution laid the foundation for the rise of civilizations, as surplus food production supported larger, more complex societies.

With the rise of civilizations came the development of writing systems, which were crucial for record-keeping, communication, and the transmission of knowledge across generations. The invention of the wheel, one of the most influential technological advancements, revolutionized transportation and trade. Wheels enabled the movement of goods and people over greater distances with less effort, facilitating cultural exchange and economic growth.

The classical civilizations of Greece and Rome made significant contributions to technology, particularly in engineering and architecture. The Romans, for instance, developed advanced road networks, aqueducts, and public buildings that showcased their engineering prowess. These innovations not only served practical purposes but also symbolized the power and sophistication of these civilizations.

The Middle Ages saw the rise of medieval technology, characterized by innovations such as the heavy plow, the windmill, and the mechanical clock. These technologies improved agricultural productivity, harnessed natural energy sources, and provided more accurate timekeeping, respectively. The period also witnessed the invention of gunpowder, which for global power dynamics.

The Renaissance marked a period of renewed interest in science and technology, driven by a spirit of inquiry and exploration. Leonardo da Vinci's sketches of flying machines and other inventions exemplified the era's innovative spirit. The invention of the printing press by Johannes Gutenberg in the 15th century was a game-changer, enabling the mass production of books and the widespread dissemination of knowledge. This democratization of information played a crucial role in the spread of ideas and the advancement of science and education.

The Industrial Revolution, which began in the late 18th century, was a watershed moment in the history of technology. The development of steam engines, mechanized looms, and other machinery revolutionized manufacturing processes, leading to unprecedented levels of production and efficiency. Factories became the new centers of economic activity, drawing people from rural areas into rapidly growing urban centers. This period also saw significant advancements in transportation, with the advent of steamships and railways, which further facilitated global trade and communication.

The 19th and early 20th centuries were marked by rapid technological progress and the rise of new industries. The invention of the telephone by Alexander Graham Bell revolutionized communication, while Thomas Edison's development of the electric light bulb extended productivity into the night. The internal combustion engine paved the way for automobiles, fundamentally changing transportation and the layout of cities. The Wright brothers' successful powered flight in 1903 opened the skies to human exploration and travel.

digital age. The development of the transistor in the 1940s paved the way for the creation of modern computers. The invention of the integrated circuit further miniaturized electronic components, making it possible to build more powerful and compact devices. The launch of the first artificial satellite, Sputnik, by the Soviet Union in 1957, and the subsequent space race, underscored the importance of technology in geopolitical competition and scientific exploration.

The advent of the personal computer in the 1970s and 1980s transformed the way people work, learn, and entertain themselves. The development of the internet in the late 20th century connected the world in unprecedented ways, enabling instant communication and access to vast amounts of information. The rise of the World Wide Web in the 1990s further democratized information and commerce, giving birth to the digital economy.

The 21st century has been characterized by rapid advancements in digital technology, including the proliferation of smartphones, the rise of social media, and the development of artificial intelligence and machine learning. These technologies have reshaped industries, from healthcare and education to entertainment and finance. The Internet of Things (IoT) has connected everyday objects to the internet, creating smart homes and cities that offer new levels of convenience and efficiency.

As we look to the future, the pace of technological change shows no signs of slowing down. Emerging technologies such as quantum computing, biotechnology, and renewable energy hold challenges, from climate change to disease. However, these advancements also raise important ethical and societal questions that must be carefully considered.

The evolution of technology is a dynamic and ongoing process, driven by human creativity and the desire to solve problems and improve lives. Each technological breakthrough builds on previous innovations, creating a complex tapestry of progress that continues to shape our world. As we navigate the future, it is essential to harness the power of technology responsibly, ensuring that it serves the greater good and enhances the human experience.

Defining Technological Innovation

Technological innovation is often heralded as the driving force behind modern progress, but what exactly constitutes this phenomenon? At its core, technological innovation encompasses the development of new technologies and the improvement of existing ones, aimed at solving problems, enhancing efficiency, or providing new capabilities. This process involves creativity, experimentation, and the application of scientific knowledge to real-world challenges. It is a dynamic interplay between inventive ideas and practical implementation, fostering advancements that can transform industries and societies.

The essence of technological innovation lies in its ability to disrupt and redefine the status quo. A prime example is the invention of the printing press by Johannes Gutenberg in the hand, a laborious and time-consuming process that limited the spread of knowledge. Gutenberg's printing press revolutionized the production of books, making them more accessible and affordable. This democratization of information played a crucial role in the Renaissance and the subsequent scientific revolution, illustrating how a single innovation can have far-reaching impacts.

Another pivotal moment in the history of technological innovation was the Industrial Revolution. This era, spanning from the late 18th to the early 19th century, saw the transition from handcrafted methods to machine-based manufacturing. Innovations such as the steam engine, mechanized spinning and weaving machines, and the power loom drastically increased production capabilities. These advancements not only boosted economic growth but also altered social structures, leading to urbanization and the rise of a new industrial working class. The ripple effects of these innovations are still felt today, as they laid the groundwork for modern industrial economies.

In the 20th century, technological innovation continued to accelerate, driven by both world wars and the subsequent Cold War. The need for advanced weaponry and strategic advantages spurred significant research and development. Technologies such as radar, jet engines, and nuclear power emerged from this period of intense innovation. Post-war, many of these technologies found civilian applications, leading to new industries and economic opportunities. For example, the development of nuclear power for energy generation has had profound implications for how we produce and consume energy.

its iterative nature. Rarely are groundbreaking technologies created in isolation; instead, they build upon previous discoveries and advancements. The development of the internet is a case in point. The concept of a global network of computers was initially explored in the 1960s with projects like ARPANET. Over the following decades, incremental innovations in networking protocols, data transmission, and user interfaces transformed this concept into the ubiquitous internet of today. Each step in this journey involved refining and expanding upon earlier work, demonstrating the cumulative nature of technological innovation.

In contemporary times, technological innovation is often associated with digital technology and the rise of the information age. The advent of personal computers, mobile devices, and the internet has revolutionized how we communicate, work, and live. Companies like Apple, Microsoft, and Google have become synonymous with innovation, continually pushing the boundaries of what is possible. The rapid pace of change in the digital realm exemplifies the concept of exponential growth, where each new development accelerates the rate of subsequent innovations.

Technological innovation is not confined to high-tech industries; it permeates all sectors of the economy. In agriculture, for instance, innovations such as genetically modified crops, precision farming, and automated machinery have significantly increased productivity and sustainability. In healthcare, advancements in medical imaging, biotechnology, and telemedicine are transforming patient care and treatment outcomes. Even traditional industries like construction are being techniques, and project management software.

One of the key drivers of technological innovation is the interplay between market demand and scientific research. Market demand provides the impetus for innovation, as companies seek to develop products and services that meet the needs and desires of consumers. Scientific research, on the other hand, provides the foundational knowledge and discoveries that fuel technological advancements. The collaboration between academia, industry, and government is crucial in fostering an environment conducive to innovation. For example, government funding for research and development can help bridge the gap between basic scientific discoveries and their practical applications.

While technological innovation has brought about tremendous benefits, it also presents challenges and ethical considerations. The rapid pace of change can lead to societal disruptions, such as job displacement due to automation. Moreover, the environmental impact of new technologies, from electronic waste to carbon emissions, must be carefully managed. Ethical considerations are particularly pertinent in fields like biotechnology and data privacy, where the implications of innovation can have profound consequences for individuals and society.

To navigate these challenges, it is essential to adopt a holistic approach to technological innovation. This involves considering not only the technical and economic aspects but also the social, environmental, and ethical dimensions. Policymakers, businesses, and researchers must work together to ensure that technological advancements are sustainable and equitable. This investing in education and retraining programs, or promoting green technologies that minimize environmental impact.

For individuals and organizations seeking to drive technological innovation, there are several practical strategies to consider. First and foremost is fostering a culture of creativity and experimentation. Innovation thrives in environments where new ideas are encouraged, and failure is seen as a learning opportunity. This can be achieved by promoting cross-disciplinary collaboration, investing in research and development, and providing resources and incentives for innovation.

Another important strategy is staying attuned to emerging trends and technologies. This involves monitoring the latest developments in relevant fields, attending industry conferences, and engaging with professional networks. By staying informed, individuals and organizations can identify opportunities for innovation and position themselves at the forefront of technological advancements.

Moreover, leveraging the power of data and analytics can significantly enhance the innovation process. Data-driven insights can help identify unmet needs, optimize product development, and improve decision-making. Investing in data infrastructure and analytical capabilities is therefore crucial for organizations looking to harness the full potential of technological innovation.

Technological innovation is a multifaceted and dynamic process that plays a central role in shaping our world. From historical breakthroughs like the printing press and the steam engine to contemporary advancements in digital technology and progress. By fostering a culture of creativity, staying informed about emerging trends, and leveraging data and analytics, individuals and organizations can continue to drive innovation and navigate the challenges and opportunities it presents. The future of technological innovation holds immense promise, and by approaching it with a holistic and responsible mindset, we can ensure that it benefits all of humanity.

Historical Milestones in Technology

Human history has been profoundly shaped by technological advancements, each milestone marking significant shifts in how societies function. The journey from simple tools to complex machinery has been long and transformative, with each era contributing its unique innovations.

In the early stages of human development, the creation of basic tools marked the beginning of technological progress. Stone tools, such as hand axes and scrapers, were among the first inventions. These tools enabled early humans to hunt, process food, and build shelters, directly impacting their survival and ability to thrive. The discovery of fire was another monumental achievement. It provided warmth, a means to cook food, and protection from predators, fundamentally altering human living conditions.

As human societies evolved, the development of agriculture around 10,000 BCE was a pivotal milestone. The ability to establishment of permanent settlements. Innovations such as the plow and irrigation systems significantly increased agricultural productivity. These advancements supported larger populations and the rise of complex societies. The agricultural revolution not only transformed human diets and lifestyles but also laid the foundation for future technological progress.

The invention of the wheel around 3500 BCE in Mesopotamia was another groundbreaking development. The wheel revolutionized transportation and trade, enabling the movement of goods and people over greater distances with ease. This innovation facilitated cultural exchange and economic growth, contributing to the prosperity of ancient civilizations. Similarly, the development of writing systems around the same time allowed for the recording and transmission of knowledge. Writing enabled the documentation of laws, trade transactions, and historical events, preserving information across generations.

The classical civilizations of Greece and Rome made significant contributions to technology, particularly in the fields of engineering and architecture. The Greeks are renowned for their advancements in mathematics and astronomy, which laid the groundwork for future scientific discoveries. The Romans, on the other hand, excelled in civil engineering. They constructed an extensive network of roads, aqueducts, and public buildings that showcased their engineering prowess. These infrastructures not only served practical purposes but also symbolized the power and sophistication of the Roman Empire.

advance in Europe, the Islamic world, and Asia. The heavy plow, introduced in the early medieval period, revolutionized agriculture in Northern Europe by making it possible to cultivate heavier, clay-rich soils. The windmill, another medieval invention, harnessed wind power for grinding grain and pumping water. These innovations increased agricultural productivity, supporting population growth and urbanization.

The invention of the mechanical clock in the 13th century represented a significant leap in timekeeping technology. Mechanical clocks provided more accurate time measurement, which was essential for various aspects of daily life, including trade, labor, and religious practices. The development of gunpowder in China during the 9th century had profound implications for warfare, changing the nature of military conflicts and altering the course of history.

The Renaissance, a period of renewed interest in science and the arts from the 14th to the 17th century, saw numerous technological advancements. Leonardo da Vinci's sketches of flying machines and other inventions exemplify the era's innovative spirit. The invention of the printing press by Johannes Gutenberg in the mid-15th century was a game-changer. The printing press enabled the mass production of books, making knowledge more accessible and fostering the spread of ideas. This democratization of information played a crucial role in the scientific revolution and the Enlightenment.

The Industrial Revolution, which began in the late 18th century, marked a major turning point in the history of technology. The development of steam engines by James Watt and others transformed manufacturing, transportation, and many other significantly increasing production efficiency. Factories became the new centers of economic activity, drawing people from rural areas into rapidly growing urban centers. Innovations such as the spinning jenny, the power loom, and the cotton gin revolutionized the textile industry, making it one of the most dynamic sectors of the time.

The 19th and early 20th centuries witnessed rapid technological progress and the rise of new industries. The invention of the telegraph and the telephone revolutionized communication, shrinking the world by allowing instant communication over long distances. Thomas Edison's development of the electric light bulb extended productivity into the night, transforming daily life and enabling the growth of cities. The internal combustion engine paved the way for automobiles, fundamentally changing transportation and the layout of cities. The Wright brothers' successful powered flight in 1903 opened the skies to human exploration and travel, setting the stage for the aviation industry.

The latter half of the 20th century saw the dawn of the digital age. The development of the transistor in the 1940s paved the way for modern computers. The invention of the integrated circuit further miniaturized electronic components, making it possible to build more powerful and compact devices. The launch of the first artificial satellite, Sputnik, by the Soviet Union in 1957, and the subsequent space race underscored the importance of technology in geopolitical competition and scientific exploration. The landing of humans on the Moon in 1969 was a monumental achievement, showcasing the potential of human ingenuity and technological prowess.

transformed how people work, learn, and entertain themselves. The development of the internet in the late 20th century connected the world in unprecedented ways, enabling instant communication and access to vast amounts of information. The rise of the World Wide Web in the 1990s further democratized information and commerce, giving birth to the digital economy. These technological advancements have had profound impacts on nearly every aspect of modern life, from education and healthcare to entertainment and commerce.

In the 21st century, technological innovation continues to advance at a rapid pace. The proliferation of smartphones, the rise of social media, and the development of advanced computing technologies have reshaped industries and societies. Innovations in biotechnology, renewable energy, and nanotechnology hold the promise of addressing some of the world's most pressing challenges, from climate change to disease. The Internet of Things (IoT) is connecting everyday objects to the internet, creating smart homes and cities that offer new levels of convenience and efficiency.

As we look to the future, the pace of technological change shows no signs of slowing down. Emerging technologies such as quantum computing, biotechnology, and renewable energy hold the promise of addressing some of the world's most pressing challenges. However, these advancements also raise important ethical and societal questions that must be carefully considered. The history of technological innovation is a testament to human ingenuity and adaptability. Each milestone has built upon previous advancements, creating a complex tapestry of progress that continues to shape our world. By understanding the historical context of these milestones, we can better appreciate challenges and opportunities that lie ahead.

The Role of Innovation in Society

Innovation has always been the catalyst for societal transformation. From the earliest human inventions to modern technological marvels, the role of innovation in shaping society cannot be overstated. It drives economic growth, enhances quality of life, and addresses complex challenges. Understanding how innovation impacts society can provide valuable insights into fostering a culture that encourages and sustains it.

Historically, innovation has been the engine of progress. Early human societies saw the development of basic tools and the harnessing of fire, which revolutionized living conditions and survival strategies. The agricultural revolution, with its introduction of farming techniques and domestication of animals, allowed for the establishment of stable communities and the rise of civilizations. These early innovations laid the groundwork for more complex societal structures and economic systems.

The Industrial Revolution exemplifies the profound impact of innovation on society. Steam engines, mechanized manufacturing, and advances in transportation transformed economies from agrarian to industrial. Factories became the new centers of production, leading to urbanization and significant social changes. People moved from rural areas to cities in search of employment, altering family structures and lifestyles. This period also saw the rise of new social classes and intricate relationship between innovation and social dynamics.

In the contemporary world, innovation continues to be a driving force behind economic development. The rise of the digital economy has created new industries and transformed existing ones. Information and communication technologies have revolutionized how businesses operate, enabling unprecedented levels of efficiency and connectivity. E-commerce, digital marketing, and remote work are just a few examples of how innovation has reshaped the economic landscape.

Moreover, innovation plays a critical role in addressing societal challenges. Healthcare advancements, for instance, have dramatically improved life expectancy and quality of life. Innovations such as vaccines, antibiotics, and medical imaging have eradicated diseases, treated previously incurable conditions, and provided early diagnosis of illnesses. The development of renewable energy technologies is another example of how innovation can tackle global issues like climate change. Solar, wind, and other renewable energy sources are reducing dependence on fossil fuels and mitigating environmental impact.

Education is another area where innovation has made significant strides. The integration of technology in classrooms has transformed teaching and learning processes. Digital tools and resources provide personalized learning experiences, making education more accessible and engaging. Online learning platforms have opened up opportunities for lifelong learning, allowing individuals to acquire new skills and knowledge at their own pace. These educational innovations changing world.

Innovation also influences cultural and social aspects of society. The proliferation of social media platforms has changed how people communicate and interact. These platforms have created new forms of socialization and community building, connecting individuals across the globe. However, they have also introduced challenges such as misinformation and privacy concerns. The impact of innovation on culture is complex, as it can both enrich and disrupt traditional social structures and norms.

To foster a culture of innovation, it is essential to create an environment that encourages creativity and risk-taking. This involves both individual and collective efforts. On an individual level, fostering curiosity and a willingness to experiment can lead to innovative ideas. Providing opportunities for interdisciplinary learning and collaboration can also spark creativity. On a collective level, organizations and governments play a crucial role in supporting innovation. This includes investing in research and development, providing funding and resources for startups, and creating policies that encourage entrepreneurship.

Furthermore, education systems must evolve to nurture innovative thinking. This includes promoting critical thinking, problem-solving skills, and an entrepreneurial mindset from an early age. Encouraging students to engage in hands-on projects and real-world problem-solving can help them develop the skills needed for innovation. Additionally, fostering a culture of lifelong learning is essential in a world where technological advancements continuously reshape industries and job markets.

of the most significant innovations have resulted from collaborative efforts. Bringing together individuals with diverse backgrounds and expertise can lead to the cross-pollination of ideas and the development of novel solutions. This is particularly important in addressing complex global challenges that require interdisciplinary approaches. Encouraging collaboration between academia, industry, and government can also accelerate the translation of research into practical applications.

Moreover, the role of leadership in fostering innovation cannot be overlooked. Leaders who prioritize innovation and create a supportive environment for it can inspire their teams to think creatively and take risks. This involves not only providing resources and support but also recognizing and rewarding innovative efforts. Creating a culture where failure is seen as a learning opportunity rather than a setback can encourage experimentation and continuous improvement.

While innovation brings numerous benefits, it also presents challenges that must be addressed. The rapid pace of technological change can lead to job displacement and economic inequality. Ensuring that the benefits of innovation are broadly shared requires proactive policies and initiatives. This includes providing retraining and upskilling opportunities for workers affected by technological advancements. Additionally, addressing ethical and social implications of innovation is crucial. This involves considering the impact of new technologies on privacy, security, and equity.

Innovation is not just about technological advancements; it also encompasses social and organizational innovations. Social and social services, can address pressing social issues and improve quality of life. Organizational innovations, including new business models and management practices, can enhance productivity and adaptability. Embracing a broad view of innovation that includes social and organizational aspects is essential in creating holistic and sustainable solutions.

The role of innovation in society is multifaceted and dynamic. It drives economic growth, addresses societal challenges, and shapes cultural and social dynamics. Fostering a culture of innovation requires creating an environment that encourages creativity, collaboration, and continuous learning. By understanding the impact of innovation and actively promoting it, societies can harness its potential to create a better future for all. The journey of innovation is ongoing, and its future holds endless possibilities for transforming our world in ways we have yet to imagine.

Overview of the Book

The journey of this book begins with an exploration of the fundamental concepts and principles that will guide you through the subsequent chapters. Each chapter builds upon the last, creating a cohesive narrative that aims to provide you with a comprehensive understanding of the subject at hand.

Starting with the basics, the initial chapters lay the groundwork by introducing key terminologies and foundational theories. These early sections are crucial as they equip you with the necessary vocabulary and conceptual frameworks that will be referenced throughout the book. For instance, understanding appreciating the current trends and future directions. By tracing the origins and development of these ideas, you gain a deeper insight into how they have shaped the present landscape.

Following the foundational chapters, the book delves into more specific areas of interest. This structured approach ensures that you do not feel overwhelmed by information, but rather, are able to digest and integrate knowledge progressively. Each chapter is designed to be a building block, adding layers of complexity and depth to your understanding. The progression from general concepts to more nuanced discussions allows for a gradual immersion into the subject, making it accessible even to those who may be new to the field.

Real-world examples and case studies are interspersed throughout the book to illustrate theoretical concepts in practical scenarios. These examples not only make the reading experience more engaging but also help in bridging the gap between theory and practice. By examining how abstract ideas are applied in real-life situations, you can better appreciate their relevance and utility. These case studies are drawn from a diverse range of contexts, ensuring a broad perspective that encompasses various applications and implications.

One of the key strengths of the book is its emphasis on practical and actionable advice. While theoretical knowledge is essential, the book recognizes the importance of equipping you with tools and strategies that can be implemented in real-world settings. Each chapter includes tips, techniques, and best practices that you can apply in your own work or studies. This pragmatic approach ensures that the knowledge gained is not just academic but also applicable and useful.

thinking and reflection. Throughout the chapters, you will encounter questions and prompts designed to stimulate your thought process and encourage deeper engagement with the material. These reflective exercises are intended to help you internalize the concepts and consider their broader implications. By thinking critically about the subject matter, you can develop a more nuanced and sophisticated understanding.

Collaboration and interdisciplinary approaches are also highlighted as important themes. The book underscores the value of drawing on diverse perspectives and expertise to address complex issues. Collaborative efforts often lead to more innovative and effective solutions, as they bring together different skill sets and viewpoints. By advocating for interdisciplinary collaboration, the book promotes a holistic approach to problem-solving.

As you progress through the chapters, you will notice a recurring emphasis on adaptability and continuous learning. The rapidly changing landscape of the subject matter necessitates a willingness to adapt and evolve. The book encourages you to stay curious and open to new ideas, as continuous learning is key to staying relevant and effective. This mindset of adaptability is crucial in navigating the challenges and opportunities that arise in the field.

Ethical considerations are woven into the narrative, acknowledging the importance of responsible and conscientious practice. Each chapter touches upon ethical issues related to the topic, prompting you to consider the moral and societal implications of your actions. By integrating ethical discussions, the book aims to cultivate a sense of responsibility and integrity.

emerging trends and potential developments. These sections provide a forward-looking perspective, encouraging you to think about the long-term trajectory of the field. By anticipating future challenges and opportunities, you can better prepare for what lies ahead. The book concludes with a synthesis of the key takeaways, reinforcing the main points and providing a cohesive summary of the journey undertaken.

In summary, this book is structured to provide a comprehensive and engaging exploration of the topic. From foundational concepts to practical applications, critical thinking exercises, and ethical considerations, each chapter is meticulously crafted to enhance your understanding and skills. Real-world examples and case studies bring the material to life, while the emphasis on adaptability and continuous learning prepares you for future challenges. Through this holistic approach, the book aims to equip you with the knowledge and tools needed to navigate and excel in the field.

Understanding Artificial Intelligence

Artificial intelligence (AI) has become a transformative force in various sectors, fundamentally altering how we approach problems, make decisions, and interact with technology. To truly understand AI, it's essential to explore its origins, how it works, and its diverse applications. This chapter aims to demystify AI by breaking down its key components and illustrating its impact through real-world examples.

AI, at its core, refers to the simulation of human intelligence in machines. These machines are programmed to think, learn, and adapt in ways that mimic human cognitive functions. The concept isn't new; it dates back to ancient myths and stories of artificial beings endowed with intelligence by their creators. However, the formal study of AI began in the mid-20th century, when pioneers like Alan Turing and John McCarthy laid its theoretical and practical foundations.

One of the fundamental aspects of AI is machine learning (ML), a subset that focuses on the development of algorithms that allow computers to learn from and make predictions based on data. Unlike traditional programming, where specific instructions are coded, ML systems are trained on large datasets. They identify patterns, learn from them, and make decisions with minimal human intervention. This ability to learn and improve over time is what makes AI so powerful and versatile.

AI. NLP enables machines to understand, interpret, and generate human language. This has led to the development of applications such as voice-activated assistants, chatbots, and translation services. The ability of AI systems to process and respond to natural language inputs has revolutionized customer service, making interactions more efficient and personalized.

AI's impact is perhaps most visible in the realm of automation. From manufacturing to healthcare, AI-driven automation has increased efficiency, reduced costs, and improved accuracy. In factories, robots powered by AI can perform repetitive tasks with precision, reducing the need for human labor and minimizing errors. In the medical field, AI algorithms can analyze medical images faster and more accurately than human doctors, aiding in early diagnosis and treatment planning.

The integration of AI in everyday life is exemplified by smart home devices. These devices use AI to learn user preferences and behaviors, adjusting settings and providing recommendations accordingly. For instance, a smart thermostat can learn your schedule and temperature preferences, optimizing energy consumption while ensuring comfort. Similarly, AI-powered security systems can detect unusual activities and alert homeowners in real-time, enhancing safety and security.

Transportation is another sector undergoing a significant transformation due to AI. Self-driving cars, once a futuristic concept, are now a reality being tested and refined. These vehicles use a combination of sensors, cameras, and AI algorithms to navigate roads, recognize obstacles, and make driving decisions. The potential benefits are immense, including increased accessibility for individuals unable to drive.

AI's role in data analysis and decision-making cannot be overstated. Businesses leverage AI to analyze vast amounts of data, uncovering insights that would be impossible for humans to detect. This data-driven approach enables companies to make informed decisions, predict market trends, and personalize customer experiences. For example, e-commerce platforms use AI to recommend products based on user behavior, enhancing customer satisfaction and driving sales.

Despite its numerous advantages, AI also presents challenges and ethical considerations. One major concern is job displacement. As AI automates tasks traditionally performed by humans, there is a fear of widespread job loss. However, it's important to view AI as a tool that can augment human capabilities rather than replace them entirely. By taking over mundane and repetitive tasks, AI allows humans to focus on more creative and complex endeavors.

Ethics in AI is a critical area of discussion. The development and deployment of AI systems must be guided by ethical principles to prevent misuse and ensure fairness. Issues such as bias in AI algorithms, data privacy, and the potential for AI to be used in harmful ways need to be addressed. Ensuring transparency in how AI systems make decisions and involving diverse perspectives in their development are steps towards building ethical AI.

Education and continuous learning are vital in the era of AI. As AI technologies evolve, so too must our skills and knowledge. Embracing lifelong learning and staying updated with advancements in AI will be crucial for individuals and incorporating AI-related subjects into their curricula, preparing students for a future where AI will be ubiquitous.

AI's potential extends to addressing global challenges. In agriculture, AI can optimize irrigation and predict crop yields, contributing to food security. In environmental conservation, AI algorithms can analyze climate data, helping to combat climate change and preserve biodiversity. By harnessing the power of AI, we can develop innovative solutions to some of the world's most pressing problems.

Collaboration and interdisciplinary approaches are essential in advancing AI. The complexity of AI systems requires expertise from various fields, including computer science, mathematics, psychology, and ethics. Collaborative efforts can lead to more robust and inclusive AI technologies. For instance, partnerships between academia, industry, and government can accelerate research and ensure that AI developments align with societal needs.

Looking ahead, the future of AI holds exciting possibilities. As technology continues to advance, AI systems will become more sophisticated and capable. Emerging areas such as quantum computing and neuromorphic engineering promise to push the boundaries of what AI can achieve. These advancements could lead to AI systems that not only perform tasks but also exhibit creativity, empathy, and a deeper understanding of the human experience.

Understanding AI is not just about grasping its technical aspects but also appreciating its broader impact on society. AI is reshaping industries, driving innovation, and presenting new opportunities and challenges. By staying informed and engaged greater good, ensuring that it serves as a force for positive change in our lives and the world at large.

In summary, AI is a multifaceted and dynamic field with far-reaching implications. Its ability to learn, adapt, and perform tasks with precision makes it a powerful tool for innovation and problem-solving. However, as we integrate AI into various aspects of our lives, it is crucial to address ethical considerations and ensure that its development is guided by principles of fairness and transparency. Embracing AI's potential while remaining mindful of its challenges will enable us to navigate the future with confidence and creativity.

AI in Everyday Life

Imagine waking up in the morning to the sound of your favorite song playing softly in the background. As you stretch and get out of bed, the lights in your room gradually brighten to mimic the rising sun, and the temperature adjusts to a comfortable level. This seemingly magical orchestration is the result of artificial intelligence seamlessly integrated into your daily routine. AI in everyday life is no longer a distant future but a present reality that enhances convenience, efficiency, and overall quality of life.

One of the most visible applications of AI in everyday life is in smart home devices. These devices, equipped with AI, learn from your habits and preferences to provide a personalized living experience. For instance, smart thermostats adjust heating and cooling based on your daily schedule and preferences, optimizing energy usage and reducing utility bills.

to voice commands, allowing you to control lights, play music, set reminders, and even order groceries without lifting a finger.

In the kitchen, AI-powered appliances are transforming how we cook and manage household chores. Refrigerators with built-in AI can track the freshness of food items, suggest recipes based on available ingredients, and even create shopping lists. Smart ovens can recognize the type of food being cooked and automatically adjust cooking times and temperatures for perfect results. These innovations not only simplify meal preparation but also help reduce food waste and promote healthier eating habits.

AI's impact extends beyond the home into our daily commutes and travel experiences. Navigation apps like Google Maps and Waze use AI to analyze real-time traffic data, providing the fastest routes and alerting drivers to potential delays. Ride-sharing services such as Uber and Lyft rely on AI algorithms to match drivers with passengers, optimize routes, and predict demand. This not only makes commuting more efficient but also reduces traffic congestion and lowers carbon emissions.

Public transportation systems are also benefiting from AI integration. In many cities, AI is used to monitor and manage transit schedules, ensuring buses and trains run on time. AI can analyze patterns in commuter behavior to optimize routes and schedules, improving overall efficiency and passenger satisfaction. Additionally, AI-powered ticketing systems streamline the process of purchasing and validating tickets, making public transportation more accessible and user-friendly.

Healthcare is another area where AI is making significant strides. Wearable devices like fitness trackers and smartwatches providing users with insights into their health and wellness. These devices often include AI algorithms that analyze the data and offer personalized recommendations for improving health outcomes. For example, a smartwatch might detect irregular heart rhythms and alert the wearer to seek medical attention, potentially saving lives.

Beyond personal health monitoring, AI is revolutionizing medical diagnostics and treatment. AI systems can analyze medical images, such as X-rays and MRIs, with remarkable accuracy, aiding in the early detection of diseases like cancer. In some cases, AI algorithms have outperformed human radiologists in identifying abnormalities. This technology is also used in genomics to identify genetic markers for various conditions, enabling personalized treatment plans tailored to an individual's genetic makeup.

Retail and e-commerce have been transformed by AI's ability to analyze consumer behavior and preferences. Online shopping platforms use AI to recommend products based on past purchases and browsing history, creating a personalized shopping experience. Chatbots and virtual assistants provide instant customer support, answering questions, and resolving issues without the need for human intervention. AI-driven inventory management systems predict demand and optimize stock levels, ensuring products are available when and where they are needed.

In the financial sector, AI is enhancing security and efficiency. Fraud detection systems use AI to analyze transaction patterns and identify suspicious activities in real-time, protecting consumers from financial crimes. AI-powered robo-advisors financial goals and risk tolerance, making financial planning more accessible. Additionally, AI is used in credit scoring to assess creditworthiness more accurately, enabling fairer lending practices.

Education is being reshaped by AI, offering new ways of learning and teaching. Adaptive learning platforms use AI to personalize educational content, adjusting the difficulty and pace based on a student's performance. This ensures that students receive the right level of challenge and support, promoting better learning outcomes. AI-driven tools also assist teachers by automating administrative tasks, such as grading and attendance tracking, allowing them to focus more on instruction and student engagement.

Entertainment and media consumption have also been revolutionized by AI. Streaming services like Netflix and Spotify use AI algorithms to recommend movies, TV shows, and music based on user preferences and viewing history. These recommendations enhance the user experience by helping people discover new content that aligns with their tastes. In gaming, AI is used to create more realistic and challenging opponents, as well as to develop immersive virtual environments.

AI's influence extends to social media, where algorithms curate content to keep users engaged. Platforms like Facebook, Twitter, and Instagram use AI to analyze user behavior and preferences, tailoring news feeds and advertisements accordingly. While this can enhance user experience by providing relevant content, it also raises concerns about privacy exposed to information that reinforces their existing beliefs.

The workplace is undergoing a transformation with AI automating routine tasks and augmenting human capabilities. In offices, AI-powered tools handle scheduling, email management, and data entry, freeing up employees to focus on more strategic and creative tasks. Recruitment processes are streamlined with AI algorithms that screen resumes and match candidates to job openings based on skills and experience. This not only speeds up hiring but also reduces bias, promoting diversity and inclusion.

Manufacturing and logistics industries are leveraging AI to optimize operations and improve efficiency. AI-driven robots and machines perform repetitive and dangerous tasks with precision, reducing the risk of injury to human workers. Predictive maintenance systems use AI to monitor equipment health and predict failures before they occur, minimizing downtime and maintenance costs. In warehouses, AI-powered systems manage inventory, track shipments, and optimize delivery routes, ensuring timely and accurate order fulfillment.

AI is also playing a crucial role in environmental conservation and sustainability efforts. Smart grids use AI to balance energy supply and demand, integrating renewable energy sources and reducing carbon emissions. AI algorithms analyze satellite imagery and sensor data to monitor deforestation, track wildlife populations, and detect environmental changes. These insights inform conservation strategies and help protect ecosystems and biodiversity.

While AI offers numerous benefits, it also presents ethical and social challenges. The potential for job displacement is a performed by humans. However, AI can also create new job opportunities and enhance existing roles by taking over mundane tasks and enabling humans to focus on more complex and creative work. Ensuring that the workforce is equipped with the skills needed to thrive in an AI-driven world is crucial.

Privacy is another critical issue as AI systems often rely on vast amounts of personal data to function effectively. Ensuring that this data is collected, stored, and used responsibly is paramount. Transparency in AI decision-making processes and accountability for outcomes are essential to building trust and preventing misuse. Addressing these ethical considerations is vital to harnessing AI's potential while safeguarding individual rights and societal values.

Understanding AI's role in everyday life is essential for navigating the modern world. By recognizing the ways in which AI enhances convenience, efficiency, and quality of life, we can better appreciate its impact and potential. Embracing AI's benefits while addressing its challenges will enable us to create a future where technology serves humanity in meaningful and responsible ways.

AI in Healthcare

Stepping into a modern hospital, one is immediately struck by the seamless interplay of technology and care. Nurses monitor patients with wearable devices, doctors consult tablets displaying real-time data, and diagnostic machines hum with precision. This transformation is driven largely by the integration of AI in healthcare, a field where digital intelligence streamline operations, and personalize medicine.

In the arena of diagnostics, AI has emerged as a powerful ally. Radiology, for example, has been revolutionized by AI algorithms capable of analyzing medical images with remarkable accuracy. These systems can detect anomalies in X-rays, MRIs, and CT scans, sometimes spotting details that human eyes might miss. This early detection capability is particularly crucial for conditions like cancer, where timely intervention can significantly improve prognosis. For instance, a study published in *Nature* demonstrated that an AI system developed for breast cancer screening outperformed radiologists in identifying cancerous lesions, reducing false positives and negatives.

Pathology, the study of disease through tissue samples, is another field where AI is making strides. Digital pathology platforms equipped with AI can analyze biopsy samples, identifying patterns and markers indicative of diseases such as cancer or autoimmune disorders. By automating these analyses, pathologists can focus on more complex cases, accelerating the diagnostic process and increasing accuracy. This not only enhances patient care but also alleviates the workload on medical professionals.

AI is also transforming the way we manage and treat chronic diseases. Diabetes, for instance, requires constant monitoring of blood glucose levels. Traditional methods involve manual logging and periodic checks, which can be cumbersome and prone to errors. AI-driven continuous glucose monitors (CGMs) now provide real-time data, alerting users to potential issues before they become critical. These devices learn from individual proactive management of the condition. Similarly, AI-powered apps offer personalized advice on diet, exercise, and medication, tailoring recommendations to each patient's unique needs.

In cardiology, AI is employed to interpret electrocardiograms (ECGs) and detect arrhythmias, heart attacks, and other cardiac conditions. These algorithms analyze the electrical activity of the heart and identify irregularities with high precision. Some wearable devices, like smartwatches, now come equipped with ECG capabilities, allowing users to monitor their heart health continuously. This proactive approach can lead to early detection and treatment of heart conditions, potentially saving lives.

Surgical procedures are another area where AI is making a significant impact. Robotic surgical systems, guided by AI, offer unparalleled precision and control. These systems can perform minimally invasive surgeries with smaller incisions, reducing recovery times and minimizing complications. AI also assists surgeons by providing real-time data and analytics during operations, enhancing decision-making and outcomes. For example, AI can help identify the best surgical path, avoiding critical structures and optimizing the surgical approach.

Personalized medicine, which tailors treatment to an individual's genetic makeup, lifestyle, and environment, is being propelled forward by AI. Genomics, the study of an individual's genes, generates vast amounts of data. AI algorithms can sift through this data to identify genetic variants linked to diseases, enabling the development of targeted therapies. This approach is particularly promising in oncology, where treatments can be increasing the efficacy and reducing side effects.

AI's role in drug discovery and development is also noteworthy. Traditional drug discovery is a time-consuming and expensive process, often taking years and billions of dollars to bring a new drug to market. AI accelerates this process by predicting how different compounds will interact with biological targets, identifying promising candidates for further testing. This not only speeds up the development of new therapies but also reduces costs, making treatments more accessible.

In primary care, AI-powered virtual assistants and chatbots are reshaping the patient experience. These tools can handle routine inquiries, schedule appointments, and provide medical advice based on symptom analysis. By triaging patients and addressing common concerns, AI frees up healthcare professionals to focus on more complex cases, improving efficiency and patient satisfaction. Additionally, telemedicine platforms equipped with AI facilitate remote consultations, expanding access to care, particularly in underserved areas.

Mental health care is another domain where AI is making a difference. AI-driven apps offer cognitive behavioral therapy (CBT) and mindfulness training, providing support for individuals dealing with anxiety, depression, and other mental health issues. These apps can track mood patterns, suggest coping strategies, and offer real-time interventions. By making mental health support more accessible and personalized, AI helps bridge the gap in mental health care, reaching those who might not have access to traditional therapy.

AI also plays a crucial role in managing healthcare operations. Predictive analytics, for example, can forecast patient ensures that hospitals and clinics are adequately prepared to handle patient influxes, reducing wait times and improving care delivery. AI-driven supply chain management systems track inventory levels and predict demand, ensuring that medical supplies and medications are always available when needed.

Ethical considerations are paramount in the integration of AI in healthcare. Ensuring patient privacy and data security is critical, given the sensitive nature of medical information. AI systems must be transparent, with clear explanations of how decisions are made, to build trust among patients and healthcare providers. Additionally, addressing biases in AI algorithms is essential to avoid disparities in care. Diverse training data and continuous monitoring are necessary to ensure that AI serves all populations equitably.

The future of AI in healthcare is promising, with ongoing advancements poised to further enhance patient care and operational efficiency. However, it is essential to approach this integration thoughtfully, balancing innovation with ethical considerations. Training healthcare professionals to work alongside AI and fostering a collaborative environment will be key to maximizing the benefits of this technology.

AI's integration into healthcare is transforming the way we diagnose, treat, and manage diseases. From early detection to personalized treatment plans, AI enhances every aspect of patient care, making it more precise, efficient, and accessible. As we continue to harness the power of AI, we must remain mindful of ethical considerations, ensuring that this technology serves all individuals fairly and responsibly. The journey towards a future where AI and human expertise work hand in hand in promising a new era of medical excellence.

The Future of AI in the Workforce

Imagine walking into an office where routine tasks are seamlessly handled by machines, allowing humans to focus on creative and strategic endeavors. This is not a scene from a distant future but an emerging reality shaped by the integration of AI in the workforce. The advent of AI is transforming industries, redefining job roles, and reshaping the skills required for the modern workplace. Understanding these changes is crucial for navigating the evolving job market and leveraging AI to enhance productivity and innovation.

In manufacturing, robots have long been a staple on assembly lines, but AI is elevating their capabilities to new heights. Factories are now equipped with smart robots that can adapt to different tasks, learn from their environment, and collaborate with human workers. These robots handle repetitive and hazardous tasks, reducing the risk of injury and freeing up human workers for more complex responsibilities. For instance, AI-driven robots can perform precision welding, quality control, and assembly with remarkable accuracy, enhancing production efficiency and product quality.

The impact of AI extends beyond the factory floor. In logistics and supply chain management, AI algorithms optimize routes, manage inventory, and predict demand with unparalleled efficiency. This ensures that products reach their destinations faster and at lower costs. Warehouse management systems powered by AI track inventory in real-time, minimizing stockouts and overstock situations. By automating these processes, companies can reduce operational costs and improve customer satisfaction.

AI is also revolutionizing the service industry. In customer service, AI-powered chatbots and virtual assistants handle routine inquiries, process transactions, and provide personalized recommendations. These tools can operate 24/7, ensuring that customers receive prompt and consistent service. Human agents, in turn, can focus on resolving complex issues that require empathy and critical thinking. This synergy between AI and human workers enhances the overall customer experience and boosts efficiency.

In healthcare, AI is transforming patient care and administrative processes. AI algorithms analyze medical records, assist in diagnosing diseases, and suggest treatment plans based on vast datasets. This not only improves diagnostic accuracy but also reduces the time doctors spend on paperwork, allowing them to focus more on patient care. Hospitals utilize AI to optimize scheduling, manage patient flow, and predict resource needs, ensuring that healthcare facilities operate smoothly and efficiently.

The financial sector is another domain where AI is making significant strides. AI-driven systems detect fraudulent transactions, assess credit risk, and provide personalized financial advice. These systems analyze vast amounts of data in real-time, identifying patterns and anomalies that might elude human analysts. By automating these tasks, financial institutions can reduce fraud, minimize risk, and offer tailored services to their clients.

workforce raises important questions about job displacement and the skills required for the future. While AI automates routine and repetitive tasks, it also creates opportunities for new roles that require advanced technical skills, creativity, and emotional intelligence. Workers need to adapt to this changing landscape by acquiring new skills and embracing lifelong learning.

One of the key skills for the future workforce is data literacy. As AI relies heavily on data, the ability to understand, interpret, and leverage data is becoming increasingly important. Workers need to be proficient in data analysis, visualization, and interpretation to make informed decisions and drive innovation. This requires familiarity with tools and platforms used for data analysis, as well as a solid understanding of statistical concepts.

Programming skills are also valuable in an AI-driven workplace. While not everyone needs to become a software engineer, a basic understanding of programming languages like Python can be beneficial. This knowledge enables workers to interact with AI systems, develop simple automation scripts, and understand the logic behind AI algorithms. Additionally, familiarity with machine learning concepts and tools can provide a competitive edge in many industries.

Critical thinking and problem-solving skills are essential as well. AI systems excel at processing vast amounts of data and identifying patterns, but human intuition and creativity are still crucial for solving complex problems. Workers need to be able to analyze situations, think critically, and develop innovative solutions that complement AI capabilities. This requires a improvement.

Emotional intelligence is another key area where humans have an advantage over machines. Jobs that involve empathy, negotiation, and relationship-building will continue to rely heavily on human skills. Workers need to develop strong interpersonal skills, the ability to understand and manage emotions, and the capacity to build trust and rapport with others. These skills are particularly important in roles that require collaboration, leadership, and customer interaction.

Lifelong learning is essential for adapting to the evolving job market. As AI technologies advance, the skills required in the workforce will continue to change. Workers need to stay updated with the latest developments, seek out new learning opportunities, and be willing to adapt their skillsets. This might involve taking online courses, attending workshops, or participating in professional development programs. Employers also play a crucial role in fostering a culture of continuous learning and providing opportunities for skill development.

The integration of AI in the workforce also necessitates ethical considerations. As AI systems make decisions that affect people's lives, it is important to ensure that these systems are fair, transparent, and accountable. Workers need to understand the ethical implications of AI, including issues related to bias, privacy, and accountability. This requires a multidisciplinary approach, combining technical knowledge with an understanding of ethics, law, and social implications.

Collaboration between humans and AI is key to maximizing the benefits of this technology. Rather than viewing AI as a threat, workers should see it as a tool that can augment their together, humans and AI can achieve outcomes that neither could accomplish alone. This requires a mindset that embraces collaboration, flexibility, and openness to new ways of working.

The future of AI in the workforce is promising, with the potential to transform industries, enhance productivity, and create new opportunities. However, it also requires workers to adapt to new roles, acquire new skills, and embrace lifelong learning. By developing data literacy, programming skills, critical thinking, emotional intelligence, and a commitment to continuous learning, workers can thrive in an AI-driven workplace. Ethical considerations and collaboration between humans and AI are also crucial for ensuring that this technology benefits society as a whole. As we navigate this changing landscape, it is essential to focus on the opportunities that AI presents and work towards a future where humans and machines work together harmoniously.

Ethical Considerations in AI

Ethical considerations in AI are a critical aspect of its development and deployment. As AI systems become increasingly integrated into various sectors, it is essential to address the ethical implications to ensure that these technologies benefit society while minimizing potential harms. Ethical issues in AI encompass a wide range of concerns, including bias, transparency, accountability, privacy, and the broader societal impacts of automation.

are trained on large datasets, which often contain historical biases. These biases can be inadvertently learned and perpetuated by AI algorithms, leading to unfair outcomes. For example, an AI-powered hiring tool might favor candidates from certain demographic groups over others, simply because the training data reflects past hiring practices that were biased. To address this, developers must implement strategies to detect and mitigate bias in AI systems. This involves carefully curating training data, using techniques such as fairness-aware machine learning, and continuously monitoring AI outputs to identify and correct biased behavior.

Transparency is another key ethical consideration. AI systems often operate as "black boxes," making decisions without providing clear explanations for their reasoning. This lack of transparency can undermine trust in AI and make it difficult to hold these systems accountable. To promote transparency, developers should strive to create AI systems that are interpretable and explainable. This can involve using simpler models that are easier to understand, providing detailed documentation of how AI systems work, and developing methods to explain AI decisions in human-understandable terms. Ensuring that stakeholders, including users and regulators, have access to clear information about how AI systems function is essential for maintaining trust and accountability.

Accountability is closely linked to transparency and is vital for addressing ethical concerns in AI. When AI systems make decisions that have significant impacts on individuals or society, it is important to establish who is responsible for those decisions. This includes determining liability when AI systems address grievances. Organizations that deploy AI systems must take responsibility for their actions and outcomes, even when those actions are mediated by AI. This can involve setting up oversight bodies, establishing clear lines of accountability, and ensuring that there are processes for auditing and reviewing AI systems.

Privacy is another major ethical concern in the context of AI. AI systems often rely on vast amounts of personal data to function effectively. This raises important questions about how that data is collected, stored, and used. Protecting individuals' privacy requires implementing robust data protection measures, such as encryption and anonymization, to prevent unauthorized access and misuse of personal information. Additionally, organizations must be transparent about their data practices, providing clear information about what data is being collected, how it will be used, and with whom it will be shared. Obtaining informed consent from individuals before collecting their data is also crucial for respecting privacy rights.

The broader societal impacts of AI and automation are also important to consider. AI has the potential to significantly disrupt labor markets by automating tasks that were previously performed by humans. While this can lead to increased efficiency and productivity, it also raises concerns about job displacement and economic inequality. To address these challenges, it is important to develop strategies for managing the transition to an AI-driven economy. This can involve investing in education and training programs to help workers acquire new skills, promoting policies that support job creation in emerging industries, and ensuring that the benefits of AI are distributed equitably across society. Additionally, fostering a build consensus on how to navigate these changes in a way that promotes social good.

Cultural and ethical diversity also play a crucial role in the development and deployment of AI. AI systems are often designed by teams that may not fully represent the diversity of the populations they serve. This can lead to AI systems that do not account for the needs and values of different cultural groups, resulting in unintended negative consequences. To address this, it is important to involve diverse stakeholders in the development of AI systems, including individuals from different cultural, geographical, and socioeconomic backgrounds. This can help to ensure that AI systems are designed in a way that is inclusive and considers the perspectives of all users.

Ethical considerations in AI also involve addressing the potential for misuse of these technologies. AI systems can be used for malicious purposes, such as creating deepfakes, conducting cyberattacks, or enabling mass surveillance. It is important to develop safeguards to prevent the misuse of AI and to establish regulations that govern the ethical use of these technologies. This can involve setting up ethical guidelines for AI development, implementing security measures to protect AI systems from malicious attacks, and promoting international cooperation to address the global nature of AI-related challenges.

Collaboration between various stakeholders is essential for addressing ethical considerations in AI. This includes cooperation between governments, industry, academia, and civil society to develop comprehensive ethical frameworks and legislation and regulations that promote ethical AI practices, while industry can contribute by adhering to ethical guidelines and best practices. Academic institutions can advance research on ethical AI and provide education and training on the ethical implications of AI technologies. Civil society organizations can advocate for the rights and interests of individuals and communities affected by AI.

Education and awareness are also crucial for promoting ethical AI. Building a broad understanding of the ethical implications of AI among developers, policymakers, and the general public can help to foster a culture of ethical responsibility. This can involve incorporating ethics into AI curricula, providing training on ethical AI practices, and raising awareness about the potential impacts of AI on society. By promoting a deeper understanding of ethical issues in AI, we can ensure that these technologies are developed and used in ways that align with societal values and promote the common good.

Ethical considerations in AI are multifaceted and require a concerted effort from all stakeholders to address. By focusing on issues such as bias, transparency, accountability, privacy, societal impacts, cultural diversity, and the potential for misuse, we can develop AI systems that are ethical and responsible. Collaborative efforts, education, and awareness are key to ensuring that AI technologies are used in ways that benefit society while minimizing potential harms. As we navigate the complexities of AI ethics, it is essential to remain vigilant and proactive in addressing these challenges, ensuring that the development and deployment of AI align with our ethical principles and societal values.

What is IoT?

The Internet of Things (IoT) refers to the interconnected network of physical devices embedded with sensors, software, and other technologies that enable them to collect and exchange data over the internet. This concept has revolutionized how we interact with our environments, from smart homes to industrial automation, creating a seamless integration between the digital and physical worlds.

Imagine waking up in the morning, and your smart thermostat has already adjusted the temperature to your preference. Your coffee maker starts brewing your favorite blend as you step into the kitchen, and your smart fridge reminds you that you're running low on milk. This level of convenience and automation is made possible by IoT. At its core, IoT involves the collection of data from various sensors and devices, which is then processed and acted upon to create a more efficient and responsive environment.

One of the fundamental aspects of IoT is the ability to gather real-time data. Sensors embedded in devices continuously monitor various parameters and relay this information to central systems. For instance, in smart cities, sensors can monitor traffic patterns and adjust traffic signals to reduce congestion. Environmental sensors can track air quality and provide real-time updates to residents. This constant flow of data allows for more informed decision-making and proactive measures.

implications for industries as well. In manufacturing, IoT enables the concept of the smart factory. Machines on the production line can communicate with each other to optimize workflows, predict maintenance needs, and reduce downtime. This level of automation and efficiency was previously unattainable, leading to significant cost savings and increased productivity.

Healthcare is another sector that has been transformed by IoT. Wearable devices such as fitness trackers and smartwatches collect data on physical activity, heart rate, and sleep patterns. This data can be shared with healthcare providers for more personalized treatment plans. Remote monitoring devices allow patients with chronic conditions to be monitored from home, reducing the need for frequent hospital visits and improving their quality of life.

The agricultural industry has also embraced IoT, leading to the rise of precision farming. By using sensors to monitor soil moisture, nutrient levels, and weather conditions, farmers can make data-driven decisions about irrigation, fertilization, and planting schedules. This not only increases crop yields but also minimizes the environmental impact of farming practices.

Despite the numerous benefits, IoT also presents several challenges. One of the primary concerns is security. With so many devices connected to the internet, the potential for cyberattacks increases significantly. Hackers can exploit vulnerabilities in IoT devices to gain unauthorized access to networks and data. Ensuring the security of IoT systems requires a multi-layered approach, including robust encryption, regular software updates, and secure authentication mechanisms.

often come from different manufacturers and use various communication protocols. Ensuring that these devices can seamlessly communicate with each other is crucial for the success of IoT ecosystems. Standardization efforts are underway, but achieving universal compatibility remains a work in progress.

Privacy is also a significant concern in the IoT landscape. With devices constantly collecting data, there is a risk of sensitive information being exposed or misused. Users need to be aware of what data is being collected and how it is being used. Transparent data policies and user consent mechanisms are essential to address these privacy concerns.

Scalability is another aspect that needs to be considered. As the number of IoT devices grows, the infrastructure supporting them must be able to handle the increased data traffic. This includes having sufficient bandwidth, storage, and processing capabilities to manage the vast amounts of data generated by IoT systems. Cloud computing and edge computing are two technologies that play a crucial role in addressing scalability issues.

Power consumption is a practical concern, especially for IoT devices deployed in remote or hard-to-reach locations. Many IoT devices rely on battery power, and ensuring long battery life is essential for their continued operation. Advances in low-power wireless communication protocols and energy-efficient hardware design are helping to address this challenge.

The potential applications of IoT are vast and varied. In the retail sector, IoT can enhance the shopping experience through smart shelves that track inventory levels and digital price tags supply chain management by providing real-time tracking of goods and optimizing delivery routes. In the energy sector, smart grids can balance energy supply and demand more efficiently, integrating renewable energy sources and reducing energy waste.

Education is another area where IoT can make a significant impact. Smart classrooms equipped with IoT devices can provide a more interactive and personalized learning experience. For example, sensors can monitor student engagement levels and adjust teaching methods accordingly. IoT can also facilitate remote learning by providing real-time access to educational resources and enabling virtual classrooms.

Public safety and emergency response can also benefit from IoT. Connected sensors can detect natural disasters such as earthquakes and floods, providing early warnings and enabling faster response times. In the event of an emergency, IoT devices can help coordinate rescue efforts by providing real-time information on the location and condition of those affected.

As we continue to explore the possibilities of IoT, it is important to consider the ethical implications of this technology. Ensuring that IoT is developed and deployed in a way that respects privacy, security, and user rights is crucial for its long-term success. Policymakers, industry leaders, and consumers must work together to create a framework that promotes innovation while safeguarding against potential risks.

The future of IoT holds immense promise. As technology continues to advance, we can expect to see even more sophisticated and integrated IoT systems that further enhance our daily lives and transform industries. By addressing the can unlock its full potential and create a more connected, efficient, and responsive world.

IoT is not just a technological advancement; it is a paradigm shift that is reshaping how we interact with our environment. From smart homes to smart cities, from healthcare to agriculture, the impact of IoT is far-reaching and transformative. Embracing this technology and addressing its challenges will be key to harnessing its benefits and ensuring a better future for all.

Smart Homes and Cities

Imagine arriving home after a long day, and your house welcoming you with perfectly adjusted lighting, a comfortable temperature, and your favorite music playing softly in the background. This vision is not futuristic; it is the reality enabled by smart homes. Smart homes integrate various devices and systems that communicate with each other to automate and optimize household activities, enhancing convenience, security, and energy efficiency.

Smart homes rely on a network of interconnected devices such as thermostats, lighting systems, security cameras, door locks, and appliances. These devices can be controlled remotely via smartphones or voice commands, thanks to the integration with digital assistants like Amazon Alexa, Google Assistant, or Apple's Siri. For example, a smart thermostat learns your daily routines and adjusts the temperature accordingly, saving energy and reducing utility bills. Similarly, smart lighting systems can be or time of day, adding both convenience and energy savings.

Security is a paramount concern for homeowners, and smart home technology offers advanced solutions to keep homes safe. Smart security cameras provide real-time video feeds that can be accessed from anywhere, giving homeowners peace of mind. Doorbell cameras not only capture footage of visitors but also allow two-way communication, making it easier to interact with delivery personnel or unexpected guests. Smart locks eliminate the need for physical keys; they can be locked or unlocked remotely, and access can be granted to family members or trusted individuals with temporary digital keys.

Energy management is another significant benefit of smart homes. Devices like smart plugs and energy monitoring systems provide insights into energy consumption, helping homeowners identify wasteful habits and optimize their energy use. For instance, smart plugs can be scheduled to turn off devices that are not in use, such as televisions or gaming consoles, reducing phantom energy consumption. Solar panels integrated with smart home systems can also optimize energy production and usage, storing excess energy in home batteries for later use.

Interoperability, or the ability of devices to work together seamlessly, is crucial for the effectiveness of smart homes. The challenge lies in the fact that different manufacturers use various communication protocols, making it difficult for devices from different brands to integrate smoothly. Efforts are underway to standardize these protocols, with initiatives like the Matter project aiming to create a unified communication standard for smart home devices. As interoperability improves, the user experience will become more seamless, with devices ecosystem.

Transitioning from individual smart homes to the broader concept of smart cities involves scaling up these technologies to enhance urban living. Smart cities use IoT technology to collect and analyze data from various sources, such as traffic sensors, environmental monitors, and public services. This data-driven approach enables city planners and administrators to make informed decisions, improving the quality of life for residents and promoting sustainable development.

Traffic management is a critical area where smart city technology can make a significant impact. By using sensors to monitor traffic flow and congestion, city authorities can optimize traffic signals and reroute traffic in real-time, reducing delays and emissions. Public transportation systems can also benefit from smart technology, with real-time tracking and scheduling information improving the reliability and convenience of buses and trains. Integrated payment systems allow residents to use a single app or card for various modes of transportation, simplifying the user experience.

Waste management is another domain where smart city technology can enhance efficiency. Smart bins equipped with sensors can monitor waste levels and optimize collection routes, ensuring that bins are emptied only when necessary. This reduces fuel consumption and emissions from waste collection vehicles while maintaining cleanliness in public spaces. Additionally, data from these systems can help city planners identify waste generation patterns and develop targeted recycling and waste reduction initiatives.

providing real-time data on air quality, noise levels, and weather conditions. This information can be used to implement policies that improve public health and environmental sustainability. For example, air quality sensors can identify pollution hotspots, allowing authorities to take targeted actions such as restricting vehicle access or increasing green spaces in those areas. Noise sensors can help enforce noise ordinances and improve the quality of life in densely populated urban areas.

Public safety is another area where smart city technology can make a substantial difference. Surveillance cameras equipped with advanced analytics can detect unusual activities and alert authorities in real-time, enabling quicker responses to incidents. Smart street lighting systems can enhance safety by adjusting brightness based on pedestrian and vehicle presence, reducing energy consumption while maintaining visibility. Emergency response systems can be integrated with smart city infrastructure to provide real-time information to first responders, improving the efficiency and effectiveness of their operations.

Citizen engagement is essential for the success of smart cities. Technology can facilitate communication between residents and city authorities, making it easier for citizens to report issues, provide feedback, and participate in decision-making processes. Mobile apps and online platforms can streamline the reporting of problems like potholes, broken streetlights, or sanitation concerns, ensuring timely resolution. Crowdsourcing data from residents can also provide valuable insights into community needs and preferences, helping city planners design more responsive and inclusive urban environments.

considerations related to privacy and data security. With the vast amount of data being collected, it is crucial to ensure that residents' personal information is protected and that data is used ethically. Transparent data policies and robust security measures are essential to maintaining public trust and safeguarding against potential breaches or misuse of information. Policymakers must strike a balance between leveraging data for urban improvement and protecting individual privacy rights.

The journey towards smart homes and cities is ongoing, with continuous advancements in technology driving new possibilities. As we embrace these innovations, it is important to consider their broader implications and strive for solutions that are inclusive, sustainable, and beneficial to all members of society. By leveraging technology to create smarter, more connected environments, we can improve the quality of life, enhance sustainability, and build resilient communities for the future.

In conclusion, smart homes and cities represent a significant evolution in how we interact with our living spaces and urban environments. The integration of technology into our daily lives offers unprecedented convenience, security, and efficiency. As we move forward, addressing challenges related to interoperability, privacy, and data security will be crucial to realizing the full potential of these advancements. By embracing a thoughtful and inclusive approach, we can harness the power of smart technology to create a better, more connected world for everyone.

IoT in Industry and Manufacturing

Manufacturing floors that once bustled with human activity are steadily evolving into automated hubs of efficiency, thanks to the Internet of Things (IoT). This transformation, often described as Industry 4.0, leverages interconnected devices to revolutionize how goods are produced, monitored, and maintained. The integration of IoT in industry and manufacturing enhances productivity, reduces downtime, and optimizes resource utilization, creating a more agile and responsive production environment.

In modern manufacturing, IoT devices are embedded in machinery, tools, and products, collecting data in real-time and transmitting it to centralized control systems. This data provides valuable insights into machine performance, production processes, and environmental conditions. For instance, sensors on a conveyor belt can monitor its speed and load, ensuring that it operates within optimal parameters. If an anomaly is detected, such as an unexpected slowdown, the system can automatically adjust or notify maintenance personnel, preventing potential bottlenecks or equipment damage.

Predictive maintenance is one of the most significant advantages IoT brings to manufacturing. Traditional maintenance schedules are often based on fixed intervals, leading to either under-maintenance or over-maintenance. IoT enables a shift to predictive maintenance by continuously monitoring equipment health and predicting when maintenance is needed. Vibration sensors on motors, for instance, can detect maintenance can be performed just in time, reducing unplanned downtime and extending the lifespan of machinery.

Inventory management also benefits from IoT integration. Smart shelves and bins equipped with weight sensors can track inventory levels in real-time. This ensures that materials and components are always available when needed, preventing production delays. Automated systems can reorder supplies before they run out, optimizing stock levels and reducing the carrying costs associated with excess inventory. Additionally, RFID tags on products and components enable precise tracking throughout the supply chain, enhancing transparency and reducing the risk of errors.

Quality control is another area where IoT has a profound impact. Sensors can monitor various parameters, such as temperature, humidity, and pressure, throughout the production process. This real-time monitoring ensures that conditions remain within specified ranges, maintaining product quality and consistency. For example, in food manufacturing, sensors can detect any deviations in temperature that might compromise product safety. Automated quality checks can identify defects early in the production process, reducing waste and rework.

The integration of IoT in manufacturing also facilitates better energy management. Factories consume significant amounts of energy, and optimizing this consumption is crucial for both cost savings and environmental sustainability. IoT devices can monitor energy usage across different processes and identify areas where energy is being wasted. Smart energy management systems can then adjust operations to reduce consumption, cooling systems. Renewable energy sources, like solar panels, can be integrated into the energy management system, further enhancing sustainability.

Worker safety is a critical concern in manufacturing, and IoT offers innovative solutions to enhance it. Wearable devices equipped with sensors can monitor workers' vital signs and environmental conditions, alerting them to potential hazards. For instance, a wearable device might detect high levels of toxic gases and warn the worker to evacuate the area. Additionally, IoT-enabled safety systems can enforce compliance with safety protocols by monitoring whether workers are wearing the necessary protective equipment and following safety procedures.

IoT also supports greater customization in manufacturing, meeting the growing demand for personalized products. Traditional mass production methods are often rigid and inflexible, but IoT enables a more adaptable approach. Flexible manufacturing systems can adjust production lines quickly to accommodate different product specifications. For example, in the automotive industry, IoT can facilitate the production of custom-configured vehicles, allowing customers to select specific features and options. This level of customization is achieved without sacrificing efficiency or increasing costs.

The successful implementation of IoT in manufacturing requires addressing several challenges. One significant challenge is ensuring data security. With numerous devices connected to a network, the potential for cyberattacks increases. Manufacturers must implement robust cybersecurity measures, including encryption, secure authentication, and regular operational integrity. Training employees on best practices for cybersecurity is also essential to mitigate risks associated with human error.

Another challenge is managing the vast amounts of data generated by IoT devices. Effective data management strategies are necessary to store, process, and analyze this data efficiently. Cloud computing solutions offer scalable storage and processing capabilities, enabling manufacturers to handle large datasets. Edge computing, which involves processing data closer to where it is generated, can reduce latency and improve real-time decision-making. Data analytics tools are crucial for extracting actionable insights from raw data, driving continuous improvement in manufacturing processes.

Interoperability is also a significant consideration. IoT devices from different manufacturers often use various communication protocols, making it challenging to create a cohesive system. Standardization efforts, such as the development of common communication protocols, are essential to ensure that devices can work together seamlessly. Manufacturers should prioritize selecting IoT solutions that are compatible with existing systems and can be easily integrated into their operations.

The workforce must also adapt to the changes brought by IoT. Employees need to develop new skills to work effectively with IoT technologies. This includes understanding how to use IoT devices, interpret data, and maintain connected systems. Ongoing training and education programs are vital to ensure that the workforce remains competent and confident in using IoT solutions. Collaboration between industry and educational institutions can help develop relevant curricula and training manufacturing.

Despite these challenges, the benefits of IoT in manufacturing are undeniable. By enhancing efficiency, reducing downtime, and enabling greater customization, IoT transforms manufacturing operations and provides a competitive edge. The ability to monitor and optimize processes in real-time leads to significant cost savings and improved product quality. Moreover, the insights gained from IoT data enable manufacturers to innovate continuously and respond to changing market demands.

The journey towards fully realizing the potential of IoT in manufacturing is ongoing. As technology advances, new opportunities will emerge, driving further improvements in efficiency, sustainability, and customization. Manufacturers that embrace IoT and invest in the necessary infrastructure, skills, and cybersecurity measures will be well-positioned to thrive in this evolving landscape. By leveraging the power of IoT, the manufacturing industry can achieve unprecedented levels of productivity, quality, and innovation, shaping the future of production for years to come.

Security Challenges in Iot

Connecting everyday devices to the internet opens up a world of convenience and efficiency, but it also exposes these devices to significant security risks. The proliferation of the Internet of Things (IoT) has introduced new vulnerabilities that can be exploited by malicious actors, making security a paramount robust security measures is crucial to safeguarding both personal and organizational data.

One of the primary security challenges in IoT is the sheer number of devices involved. Unlike traditional computing environments, IoT ecosystems can consist of thousands, if not millions, of interconnected devices. Each device represents a potential entry point for cyberattacks. Many IoT devices are designed with limited computing power and memory, which often results in minimal security features. Manufacturers frequently prioritize cost and speed to market over security, leading to devices that are inherently vulnerable.

The diversity of IoT devices further complicates security efforts. These devices range from simple sensors to complex industrial machines, each with different operating systems, communication protocols, and security capabilities. This heterogeneity makes it difficult to develop a one-size-fits-all security strategy. Ensuring that all devices within an IoT ecosystem are secure requires tailored approaches that consider the specific characteristics and constraints of each device.

Another significant challenge is the lack of standardized security protocols. The IoT industry is still relatively young, and many devices use proprietary communication protocols that are not compatible with others. This lack of standardization hinders the development of comprehensive security solutions that can be universally applied. Efforts are underway to establish standard security frameworks, but the rapid pace of IoT adoption means that many devices are already in use without adequate security measures.

IoT devices. Many devices come with default usernames and passwords that are rarely changed by users. These default credentials are often well-known and easily exploitable by attackers. Even when unique credentials are used, they may not be sufficiently complex to prevent unauthorized access. Implementing strong, unique authentication for each device is essential to prevent unauthorized access and control.

Data encryption is another critical aspect of IoT security that is frequently overlooked. Data transmitted between IoT devices and central systems is often sent in plain text, making it vulnerable to interception and tampering. Encrypting data both in transit and at rest is crucial to protect sensitive information from eavesdropping and unauthorized access. However, the limited processing power of many IoT devices can make implementing robust encryption challenging.

Firmware updates present a dual-edged sword in IoT security. On one hand, regular updates are necessary to patch vulnerabilities and improve security. On the other hand, the process of updating firmware can itself be a security risk if not properly managed. Unauthorized firmware updates can introduce malicious code into devices, compromising their security. Secure update mechanisms that authenticate and verify the integrity of updates are essential to ensure that only legitimate updates are applied.

The interconnected nature of IoT devices means that a single compromised device can pose a threat to the entire network. Attackers can use one vulnerable device as a foothold to launch attacks on other devices within the network. Network segmentation is a vital strategy to mitigate this risk. By isolating compromised device can be contained, preventing the spread of malware and other malicious activities.

Physical security is another often-overlooked aspect of IoT security. Many IoT devices are deployed in locations where they are easily accessible to unauthorized individuals. Physical tampering can compromise the integrity of the device and the data it collects. Ensuring that devices are physically secure, whether through tamper-evident seals or secure enclosures, is crucial to preventing unauthorized access and manipulation.

Endpoint security solutions, such as firewalls and intrusion detection systems, are essential for protecting IoT devices and networks. These solutions monitor network traffic for signs of suspicious activity and can block malicious attempts to access or control devices. However, traditional endpoint security solutions may not be suitable for all IoT devices due to their limited resources. Lightweight security solutions that are specifically designed for IoT environments are needed to provide adequate protection without overburdening the devices.

User education and awareness are critical components of IoT security. Many security breaches occur due to human error, such as using weak passwords or failing to apply updates. Educating users about the importance of security best practices and how to implement them can significantly reduce the risk of security incidents. This includes training on how to recognize phishing attempts, the importance of regular updates, and the use of strong, unique passwords for each device.

Regulatory compliance is becoming increasingly important in the realm of IoT security. Governments and regulatory bodies are starting to recognize the need for standardized security measures and are introducing regulations to ensure that IoT devices meet minimum security standards. Compliance with these regulations is not only a legal requirement but also helps to establish a baseline level of security across the industry. Manufacturers and users alike must stay informed about relevant regulations and ensure that their devices and practices comply with these standards.

The future of IoT security will likely involve a combination of technological advancements and regulatory measures. Advances in machine learning and artificial intelligence can help to identify and respond to threats more quickly and accurately. Automated security solutions that can adapt to evolving threats will be essential in managing the complexity and scale of IoT ecosystems. At the same time, continued efforts to develop and enforce standardized security protocols will be crucial in ensuring a consistent level of security across all IoT devices.

In summary, the security challenges in IoT are multifaceted and require a comprehensive approach that includes strong authentication, data encryption, secure firmware updates, network segmentation, physical security, endpoint protection, user education, and regulatory compliance. As the IoT landscape continues to evolve, staying ahead of emerging threats and adopting best practices for security will be essential to protect both individual devices and the broader network. By addressing these challenges proactively, we can harness the full potential of IoT while safeguarding against the risks it introduces.

Introduction to Blockchain Technology

Imagine a world where transactions can be verified without a trusted third party, where data is immutable and transparent, and where trust is built into the very fabric of technology. This is the promise of blockchain technology, a revolutionary system that has the potential to transform industries from finance to healthcare. At its core, blockchain is a decentralized ledger that records transactions across multiple computers, ensuring that the record is secure and cannot be altered retroactively.

Blockchain technology was first conceptualized in 2008 by an anonymous person or group known as Satoshi Nakamoto, primarily as the underlying technology for Bitcoin. However, the applications of blockchain extend far beyond cryptocurrencies. To understand blockchain, it's essential to grasp its fundamental components: blocks, chains, and the mechanisms that secure them.

A blockchain is composed of a series of blocks, each containing a list of transactions. These blocks are linked together in chronological order, forming a chain. Each block has a unique identifier called a hash, which is generated based on the data within the block and the hash of the previous block. This interlinking of hashes is what makes blockchain secure; altering the information in one block would require changing all subsequent blocks, an almost impossible task due to the computational power required.

Unlike traditional databases that are managed by a central authority, a blockchain is maintained by a network of nodes, each holding a copy of the entire ledger. This distributed nature ensures that no single entity has control over the entire system, making it resistant to censorship and fraud. When a new transaction is proposed, it must be verified by the network through a consensus mechanism before it is added to the blockchain.

There are several consensus mechanisms used in blockchain technology, with Proof of Work (PoW) and Proof of Stake (PoS) being the most common. PoW, used by Bitcoin, requires nodes to solve complex mathematical puzzles to validate transactions and add them to the blockchain. This process, known as mining, is energy-intensive but ensures the integrity and security of the network. PoS, on the other hand, selects validators based on the number of tokens they hold and are willing to "stake" as collateral. PoS is considered more energy-efficient and scalable compared to PoW.

Smart contracts are another revolutionary aspect of blockchain technology. These are self-executing contracts with the terms of the agreement directly written into code. Smart contracts automatically enforce and execute the terms when predefined conditions are met, eliminating the need for intermediaries. For example, in a supply chain scenario, a smart contract could automatically release payment once goods are delivered and verified, reducing delays and the potential for fraud.

The transparency and immutability of blockchain make it particularly valuable in industries where trust and verification are paramount. In the financial sector, blockchain can costs and increasing transaction speed. By eliminating the need for intermediaries like banks, transactions can be completed in minutes rather than days. Furthermore, the transparency of the ledger reduces the risk of fraud and money laundering.

Supply chain management is another area where blockchain can have a significant impact. By recording every step of a product's journey on a blockchain, companies can provide verifiable proof of origin, ensuring authenticity and ethical sourcing. This transparency helps to build trust with consumers and partners, as they can trace the entire lifecycle of a product. Additionally, in the case of recalls, blockchain enables quick identification of affected batches, minimizing harm and reducing costs.

Healthcare is also poised to benefit from blockchain technology. Patient records stored on a blockchain can be securely shared between healthcare providers, ensuring continuity of care while protecting patient privacy. The immutability of blockchain ensures that medical records cannot be tampered with, providing a reliable source of truth. Moreover, blockchain can streamline the management of pharmaceutical supply chains, preventing counterfeit drugs from entering the market and ensuring that medications are stored and transported under proper conditions.

Despite its many advantages, blockchain technology is not without challenges. Scalability is a significant concern, especially for public blockchains like Bitcoin and Ethereum that require every node to process every transaction. This can lead to slow transaction speeds and high fees during periods of high demand. Various solutions are being explored to address this issue, such as sharding, which involves splitting the blockchain like the Lightning Network, which enable off-chain transactions that are later settled on the main blockchain.

Another challenge is the regulatory landscape. Blockchain operates across borders, often in a regulatory grey area. Governments and regulatory bodies are still grappling with how to classify and regulate blockchain-based assets and activities. Clear and consistent regulations are needed to provide certainty for businesses and protect consumers without stifling innovation. As the technology matures, it is likely that we will see more comprehensive regulatory frameworks emerge.

Interoperability between different blockchain networks is another hurdle to widespread adoption. Currently, many blockchains operate in silos, unable to communicate with each other. This fragmentation limits the potential of blockchain technology. Efforts are underway to develop interoperability protocols that will enable different blockchains to interact seamlessly, creating a more connected and efficient ecosystem.

The energy consumption of blockchain, particularly those using PoW, has also raised environmental concerns. The computational power required for mining consumes a significant amount of electricity, contributing to carbon emissions. Transitioning to more energy-efficient consensus mechanisms like PoS and exploring renewable energy sources for mining operations are critical steps towards mitigating the environmental impact of blockchain technology.

As blockchain technology continues to evolve, it holds the promise of transforming not only financial systems but also a wide range of industries by enhancing transparency, security, and efficiency. Embracing this technology requires a careful to address its challenges. By understanding the principles and potential of blockchain, individuals and organizations can position themselves at the forefront of this digital revolution, harnessing its power to create more trustworthy and efficient systems. With continued development and collaboration, blockchain technology can pave the way for a more transparent and decentralized future.

How Cryptocurrencies Work

Cryptocurrencies have revolutionized the way we perceive and handle money, offering a decentralized alternative to traditional financial systems. At the heart of this revolution is the concept of digital currencies that operate on a technology known as blockchain. To truly understand how cryptocurrencies work, one must delve into the intricacies of blockchain technology, mining, wallets, and the mechanisms that ensure security and trust in a decentralized environment.

Cryptocurrencies are digital or virtual currencies that use cryptography for security. Unlike traditional currencies issued by governments and central banks, cryptocurrencies are typically decentralized and operate on a technology called blockchain. Bitcoin, introduced in 2009 by an anonymous entity known as Satoshi Nakamoto, was the first cryptocurrency and remains the most well-known. However, thousands of other cryptocurrencies, often referred to as altcoins, have since emerged, each with unique features and uses.

At the core of any cryptocurrency is the blockchain, a decentralized ledger that records all transactions across a which is then added to a chain of previous blocks, hence the term blockchain. This chain of blocks is maintained by a network of nodes, which are computers that participate in the network by validating and relaying transactions. The decentralized nature of blockchain ensures that no single entity has control over the entire network, making it resistant to censorship and fraud.

The process of adding new transactions to the blockchain is known as mining. Mining involves solving complex mathematical problems that require significant computational power. Miners compete to solve these problems, and the first one to do so gets to add the new block to the blockchain. As a reward for their efforts, miners receive newly created cryptocurrency tokens, as well as transaction fees from the transactions included in the block. This process not only secures the network but also introduces new tokens into circulation.

While Bitcoin uses a Proof of Work (PoW) consensus mechanism, which requires miners to perform energy-intensive calculations, other cryptocurrencies use different mechanisms. Proof of Stake (PoS), for instance, selects validators based on the number of tokens they hold and are willing to "stake" as collateral. PoS is more energy-efficient compared to PoW and is being adopted by many newer cryptocurrencies. Another mechanism, Delegated Proof of Stake (DPoS), involves token holders voting for a small number of delegates who validate transactions on their behalf, further enhancing efficiency.

To interact with a cryptocurrency network, users need a digital wallet. A wallet is a software application that allows users to store, send, and receive cryptocurrencies. Each wallet has a pair wallet address that others use to send cryptocurrencies to, and a private key, which is known only to the owner and is used to sign transactions. The private key must be kept secure because anyone with access to it can control the funds in the wallet.

Transactions in a cryptocurrency network involve transferring tokens from one wallet to another. When a user initiates a transaction, it is broadcast to the network and awaits validation by miners or validators, depending on the consensus mechanism. Once validated, the transaction is included in a new block and added to the blockchain. The transaction is then considered confirmed, and the tokens are transferred from the sender's wallet to the recipient's wallet. This process typically takes a few minutes, although the exact time can vary depending on network congestion and the specific cryptocurrency.

One of the most significant advantages of cryptocurrencies is their potential to provide financial services to the unbanked and underbanked populations. Traditional banking systems often exclude individuals who lack access to banking infrastructure or necessary documentation. Cryptocurrencies, on the other hand, require only an internet connection and a digital wallet, making them accessible to anyone, anywhere in the world. This inclusivity can empower individuals in developing countries by providing them with tools for saving, investing, and transacting without reliance on traditional banks.

However, the world of cryptocurrencies is not without risks and challenges. One major concern is the volatility of cryptocurrency prices. Unlike traditional currencies, which are typically stable and backed by governments, cryptocurrencies can experience significant price fluctuations in short periods. This volatility can be attributed to various factors, including market speculation, regulatory news, technological developments, and macroeconomic trends. Investors in cryptocurrencies must be prepared for the potential for high returns as well as substantial losses.

Security is another critical issue in the cryptocurrency space. While the underlying blockchain technology is secure, the platforms and applications built on top of it can be vulnerable to hacks and exploits. Numerous high-profile incidents have resulted in the loss of millions of dollars worth of cryptocurrencies. To mitigate these risks, users must adopt best practices for securing their digital wallets, such as using hardware wallets, enabling two-factor authentication, and regularly updating their software.

Regulation is a topic of ongoing debate in the cryptocurrency community. Cryptocurrencies operate in a decentralized and often anonymous environment, which can complicate regulatory oversight. Governments around the world are grappling with how to regulate cryptocurrencies to protect consumers and prevent illegal activities such as money laundering and fraud, while also fostering innovation. The regulatory landscape varies significantly from country to country, with some embracing cryptocurrencies and blockchain technology, while others impose strict regulations or outright bans.

Despite these challenges, cryptocurrencies continue to gain traction and acceptance. Major companies are beginning to accept cryptocurrencies as payment, and institutional investors are increasingly adding digital assets to their portfolios.

Additionally, central banks are exploring the concept of central bank digital currencies (CBDCs), which are digital versions of traditional currencies that leverage blockchain technology. These developments indicate a growing recognition of the potential of cryptocurrencies and blockchain technology to transform the financial landscape.

Educational resources and communities play a vital role in helping beginners navigate the complex world of cryptocurrencies. Numerous online courses, forums, and social media groups are dedicated to educating individuals about the fundamentals of cryptocurrencies, investment strategies, and security best practices. Engaging with these resources can help newcomers build a solid understanding and make informed decisions.

The future of cryptocurrencies is both exciting and uncertain. As technology continues to evolve, we can expect to see new innovations that address current limitations and open up new possibilities. Layer two solutions, such as the Lightning Network for Bitcoin, aim to improve scalability and reduce transaction fees. Interoperability protocols seek to enable seamless communication between different blockchain networks, enhancing the overall ecosystem. Moreover, advancements in privacy-focused cryptocurrencies and technologies could provide enhanced confidentiality for users.

In conclusion, cryptocurrencies represent a groundbreaking shift in how we think about and use money. By leveraging blockchain technology, they offer a decentralized, secure, and accessible alternative to traditional financial systems. Understanding how cryptocurrencies work, from blockchain and mining to wallets and transactions, is essential for anyone such as volatility, security risks, and regulatory uncertainties exist, the potential benefits of cryptocurrencies are vast, promising to democratize financial services and empower individuals worldwide. As we move forward, staying informed and engaged with the latest developments will be crucial in navigating the ever-evolving world of cryptocurrencies.

Blockchain Beyond Finance

Blockchain technology, initially developed to support cryptocurrencies like Bitcoin, has proven to be a versatile tool with applications far beyond the financial sector. Its core features—decentralization, immutability, and transparency—make it suitable for various industries, including supply chain management, healthcare, voting systems, and intellectual property protection. Exploring these applications reveals the transformative potential of blockchain technology and its ability to address long-standing challenges across different domains.

Supply chain management is one of the most promising areas for blockchain application. Traditional supply chains often suffer from inefficiencies, lack of transparency, and fraud. By using blockchain, companies can create an immutable ledger of all transactions and movements of goods. This transparency allows all parties involved—from manufacturers to end consumers—to trace the origin and journey of a product. For example, a blockchain-based system can track a product from its raw material stage through production, shipping, and finally to the store shelf. This not only enhances trust among participants but counterfeit goods and unethical practices in sourcing materials.

In the healthcare sector, blockchain can revolutionize the way patient data is managed and shared. Currently, patient records are often fragmented across different systems and providers, making it difficult to obtain a comprehensive view of a patient's medical history. Blockchain offers a solution by providing a secure, unified, and tamper-proof record that can be accessed by authorized healthcare providers. This ensures that patient data is accurate, up-to-date, and easily shareable, leading to better diagnosis and treatment. Additionally, blockchain can enhance the security of sensitive medical information, reducing the risk of data breaches and unauthorized access.

Voting systems are another critical area where blockchain technology can make a significant impact. Traditional voting systems are often plagued by issues such as voter fraud, tampering, and lack of transparency. Blockchain can address these problems by providing a secure and transparent platform for recording votes. Each vote can be recorded as a transaction on the blockchain, ensuring that it is immutable and verifiable. This not only enhances the integrity of the voting process but also increases voter confidence in the system. Furthermore, blockchain-based voting can facilitate remote voting, making it more accessible to people who are unable to vote in person due to various reasons.

Intellectual property protection is another domain where blockchain can offer substantial benefits. Creators of digital content, such as artists, musicians, and writers, often struggle to protect their work from unauthorized use and piracy. Blockchain can provide a solution by enabling the creation of a intellectual property. This ledger can be used to prove ownership and track the distribution and usage of digital content. Smart contracts, which are self-executing contracts with the terms directly written into code, can be used to automate license agreements and ensure that creators are fairly compensated for their work.

Blockchain's potential extends to the real estate industry as well. Property transactions are traditionally complex and involve numerous intermediaries, which can lead to delays and increased costs. Blockchain can streamline the process by providing a transparent and secure platform for recording property ownership and transactions. This can reduce the need for intermediaries, speed up the transaction process, and lower costs. Furthermore, blockchain can help prevent fraud by providing a tamper-proof record of property ownership, making it easier to verify the legitimacy of property titles.

The energy sector is another field where blockchain technology can drive innovation. With the growing emphasis on renewable energy and decentralized power generation, blockchain can facilitate peer-to-peer energy trading. Homeowners with solar panels, for example, can use blockchain to sell excess energy to their neighbors. Blockchain provides a transparent and secure platform for recording energy transactions, ensuring that all parties are fairly compensated. Additionally, blockchain can enhance the efficiency of energy grids by providing real-time data on energy production and consumption, enabling better management of energy resources.

Blockchain can also play a crucial role in enhancing the transparency and efficiency of charitable organizations. Donors whether they reach the intended beneficiaries. By using blockchain, charities can provide a transparent record of all donations and their allocation. Donors can trace their contributions from the moment they are made to their final use, ensuring that funds are used appropriately and effectively. This transparency can increase trust in charitable organizations and encourage more people to donate.

The potential of blockchain technology is not limited to the aforementioned applications. It can also be used in areas such as identity verification, digital voting, and the Internet of Things (IoT). For instance, blockchain can provide a secure and decentralized platform for verifying identities, reducing the risk of identity theft and fraud. In the IoT space, blockchain can enhance the security and interoperability of connected devices, enabling them to communicate and transact with each other in a secure and transparent manner.

Despite its potential, the adoption of blockchain technology faces several challenges. One of the main hurdles is scalability. Many blockchain networks, such as Bitcoin and Ethereum, struggle to handle a large number of transactions simultaneously, leading to delays and increased costs. Efforts are being made to address these issues through the development of new consensus mechanisms, layer-two solutions, and other scalability enhancements.

Another challenge is regulatory uncertainty. The regulatory environment for blockchain and cryptocurrencies is still evolving, and there is often a lack of clarity on how existing laws apply to blockchain-based activities. This uncertainty can hinder the adoption of blockchain technology, as businesses and without clear regulatory guidance. Governments and regulatory bodies around the world are working to develop frameworks that balance the need for regulation with the potential for innovation.

Interoperability is another critical issue that needs to be addressed for blockchain technology to achieve widespread adoption. Currently, there are numerous blockchain platforms, each with its own protocols and standards. This fragmentation makes it difficult for different blockchain networks to communicate and interact with each other. Efforts are being made to develop interoperability solutions that enable seamless communication between different blockchains, enhancing the overall ecosystem and enabling more complex and integrated applications.

In conclusion, blockchain technology holds immense potential beyond its initial application in cryptocurrencies. Its features of decentralization, immutability, and transparency make it suitable for a wide range of industries, from supply chain management and healthcare to voting systems and intellectual property protection. While there are challenges to overcome, such as scalability, regulatory uncertainty, and interoperability, the ongoing advancements and innovations in the field are paving the way for broader adoption. As more industries recognize the value of blockchain and integrate it into their operations, we can expect to see significant improvements in efficiency, transparency, and security across various domains.

Navigating the regulatory and legal landscape of emerging technologies presents significant challenges, and blockchain technology is no exception. The decentralized nature of blockchain, which offers immense potential for innovation and efficiency, also creates a unique set of legal and regulatory issues that must be addressed to ensure its safe and widespread adoption. Understanding these challenges is crucial for developers, businesses, and policymakers as they work together to integrate blockchain into various sectors.

One of the primary regulatory challenges facing blockchain technology is the classification of digital assets. Whether a digital asset is classified as a security, commodity, or currency has profound implications for how it is regulated. For instance, in the United States, the Securities and Exchange Commission (SEC) has taken the position that many digital tokens constitute securities and are thus subject to federal securities laws. This classification requires token issuers to comply with stringent registration and disclosure requirements, which can be burdensome for startups and small businesses. On the other hand, the Commodity Futures Trading Commission (CFTC) treats certain digital assets like Bitcoin as commodities, subjecting them to different regulatory standards. This lack of a unified approach leads to regulatory uncertainty, which can stifle innovation and deter investment in blockchain projects.

Moreover, the global nature of blockchain technology adds another layer of complexity. Different countries have varying jurisdiction may be prohibited in another. This fragmented regulatory environment poses significant challenges for blockchain projects that operate across borders. Companies must navigate a maze of regulations, which can be both time-consuming and costly. For instance, while some countries like Switzerland and Singapore have adopted blockchain-friendly regulations to attract innovation, others have imposed strict restrictions or outright bans on certain blockchain activities. This inconsistency can hinder the growth of global blockchain networks and complicate compliance efforts.

Privacy and data protection regulations also pose significant challenges for blockchain technology. The immutable nature of blockchain, which ensures that data cannot be altered or deleted, conflicts with data protection laws that grant individuals the right to have their personal data erased. The European Union's General Data Protection Regulation (GDPR) is a prime example. GDPR mandates that individuals have the "right to be forgotten," which is difficult to reconcile with blockchain's permanence. Developers must find ways to balance the benefits of immutability with compliance to privacy regulations, potentially through innovative solutions such as zero-knowledge proofs or off-chain storage.

Smart contracts, which are self-executing contracts with the terms directly written into code, introduce another set of legal challenges. These contracts operate automatically when predefined conditions are met, without the need for intermediaries. While this can increase efficiency and reduce costs, it also raises questions about enforceability and liability. Traditional legal frameworks are not well-equipped to handle disputes arising from smart contracts, and there is often no contract contains a coding error that leads to unintended consequences, it is unclear who would be held liable. Legal systems need to evolve to address these issues and provide clarity on the legal status of smart contracts.

The issue of jurisdiction is also a significant challenge in the blockchain space. Given that blockchain networks are decentralized and often spread across multiple jurisdictions, it can be difficult to determine which legal system has authority over a particular transaction or dispute. This lack of clarity can complicate enforcement actions and create legal uncertainty. For example, if a blockchain-based transaction involves parties in different countries, it is not always clear which country's laws apply or which courts have jurisdiction. This can lead to complex legal battles and increased costs for all parties involved.

Regulatory bodies are also grappling with the potential for blockchain technology to facilitate illicit activities such as money laundering, terrorist financing, and fraud. The pseudonymous nature of many blockchain transactions can make it difficult to trace the flow of funds and identify the parties involved. To address these concerns, regulators are increasingly requiring blockchain projects to implement robust Know Your Customer (KYC) and Anti-Money Laundering (AML) measures. These requirements can add significant compliance burdens for blockchain businesses, particularly those operating in multiple jurisdictions with differing standards. However, they are essential for ensuring the integrity of the financial system and preventing misuse of the technology.

Taxation is another area where blockchain technology presents regulatory challenges. Tax authorities around the world are still based transactions. The decentralized nature of blockchain and the use of cryptocurrencies complicate the tracking and reporting of taxable events. For example, determining the value of a cryptocurrency transaction at the time it occurs can be challenging due to the volatility of digital asset prices. Additionally, the use of decentralized exchanges and peer-to-peer transactions can make it difficult for tax authorities to monitor and enforce compliance. Clear and consistent tax guidelines are needed to provide certainty for taxpayers and ensure proper tax collection.

Despite these challenges, there are ongoing efforts to create a more supportive regulatory environment for blockchain technology. Regulatory sandboxes, for instance, allow blockchain projects to operate in a controlled environment under the supervision of regulators. This enables innovators to test their solutions without the full burden of regulatory compliance, while regulators gain insights into emerging technologies. Such initiatives can foster innovation while ensuring that regulatory frameworks evolve in step with technological advancements.

International cooperation is also essential for addressing the regulatory and legal challenges of blockchain technology. Given the borderless nature of blockchain, coordinated efforts among countries can help create consistent regulatory standards and facilitate cross-border transactions. Organizations such as the Financial Action Task Force (FATF) are working to establish global guidelines for regulating digital assets and blockchain activities. Collaborative efforts can help harmonize regulations, reduce compliance burdens, and support the growth of a global blockchain ecosystem.

potential for transforming various industries, it also presents significant regulatory and legal challenges. The classification of digital assets, global regulatory fragmentation, privacy concerns, smart contract enforceability, jurisdictional issues, illicit activity prevention, and taxation all require careful consideration and innovative solutions. As blockchain technology continues to evolve, so too must the regulatory frameworks that govern it. Through collaboration, innovation, and adaptive regulation, it is possible to create an environment that fosters the growth of blockchain technology while addressing the associated legal and regulatory challenges.

9 798330 314348